AN

ACCOUNT OF THE PROCEEDINGS

PRELIMINARY TO THE ORGANIZATION

OF THE

Massachusetts Institute of Technology;

WITH A

LIST OF THE MEMBERS THUS FAR ASSOCIATED,

AND

AN APPENDIX,

CONTAINING PETITIONS AND RESOLUTIONS IN AID OF THE OBJECTS OF THE COMMITTEE OF ASSOCIATED INSTITUTIONS OF SCIENCE AND ART.

BOSTON:
PRINTED BY JOHN WILSON AND SON,
22, SCHOOL STREET.
1861.

AN

ACCOUNT OF THE PROCEEDINGS

PRELIMINARY TO THE ORGANIZATION

OF THE

Massachusetts Institute of Technology;

WITH A

LIST OF THE MEMBERS THUS FAR ASSOCIATED,

AND

AN APPENDIX,

CONTAINING PETITIONS AND RESOLUTIONS IN AID OF THE OBJECTS OF THE COMMITTEE OF ASSOCIATED INSTITUTIONS OF SCIENCE AND ART.

BOSTON:
PRINTED BY JOHN WILSON AND SON,
22, School Street.
1861.

PROCEEDINGS.

The Committee of Associated Institutions of Science and Art, in their memorial to the last Legislature (House Doc. 13), indicated in a brief and general form the claims of Industrial Science and Practical Education as leading objects in the plan of collocated institutions, for which they asked a reservation of certain of the Back-Bay lands. As, however, no definite organization had been framed embracing these great interests in a practical shape, the Committee were satisfied for the time with resting their argument in behalf of this part of their plan upon the obvious public importance of such enlarged means of practical instruction in the Arts and Applied Sciences as were suggested, and upon an assured conviction that the community would liberally co-operate in any wisely methodized scheme for promoting them.

Believing that the failure of their previous appeal to the Legislature was, in part at least, due to the incompleteness and vagueness in which they had presented this department of their general plan; and finding, that, in spite of their ill success, an earnest and increasing interest was very generally felt for the establishment of an Institution devoted to Industrial Science and Education, — the Committee determined on taking such steps as were practicable towards the organization, in a preliminary form, of an Institution of this character.

Accordingly, at a meeting held May 28, 1860, the Committee assigned to a Subcommittee, consisting of W. B. Rogers, E. B. Bigelow, J. M. Beebe, M. D. Ross, and C. H. Dalton, the duty of preparing and reporting the plan of an Institution designed for the advancement of the Industrial Arts and Sciences and Practical Education in the Commonwealth.

In fulfilment of this purpose, a scheme of organization was framed by the Chairman, and embodied in a Report, presenting, in some detail and comprehensiveness, the "Objects and Plan of an Institute of Technology, including a Society of Arts, a Museum of Arts, and a School of Industrial Science." This Report, accepted by the General Committee, was read by the Chairman at a public meeting of gentlemen interested in the subject, held by appointment, at the Rooms of the Board of Trade, on the 5th of October, 1860; and, on vote, was approved, and its publication recommended.

Thus sanctioned, the pamphlet, setting forth the objects and plan of the proposed Institute of Technology, was distributed through the City and State among persons who were thought most likely to be interested in the subjects to which it relates; and, in order to elicit the opinions and invite the co-operation of those best qualified to judge of the practical merits of the plan, the pamphlet was accompanied by the following circular:—

BOSTON, November, 1860.

DEAR SIR,—In sending you the accompanying pamphlet, setting forth the objects and plan of an Institute of Technology proposed to be established, if practicable, on the Back-Bay lands in Boston, we beg to request that you will give it your early and thoughtful attention.

In our view of the great advantages which the industrial interests and practical education of the Commonwealth would derive from such an Institution, we cannot but hope that our plan will so approve itself to your judgment as to win your sympathy and active co-operation.

It is proposed, at an early day, to hold a meeting in this city for the purpose of adopting measures preliminary to the organization of the Institute. Of this you will be duly notified; and we trust that your interest in the subject will secure us the benefit of your presence on the occasion. Meanwhile, it will give us great pleasure to be allowed to number you among the prospective members of the Institute, and to have the influence and authority of your name, as well as the advantage of your counsel, in connection with the undertaking.

Should it be your wish to unite with us, please indicate the class of subjects, as mentioned under the heads of "Committees of Arts," in which you would feel most directly interested; addressing your reply to the undersigned.

William B. Rogers, *Chairman of Committee.*

The numerous responses to this circular, approving the objects and plan of the proposed Institute, and offering co-operation in its several departments as laid down in the Report, satisfied the Committee that its leading features were practically suited to the great industrial and educational objects in view, and that the general scheme was likely to command the hearty and helpful approval of the community at large.

After an interval of about two months from the distribution of the pamphlet, the Committee proceeded to call a meeting for the purpose of effecting a preliminary organization of the Institute, confining the invitation to those only to whom the Report had previously been sent, and who were supposed to have made themselves acquainted with the different features and bearings of the plan thus distinctly submitted to them. It will be seen that the following circular, calling this meeting, was framed with the view of testing still further the deliberate approbation and interest which might be felt in regard to the proposed Institution: —

BOSTON, Jan. 7, 1861.

DEAR SIR, — You have been made acquainted, through the pamphlet and circular which have been addressed to you, with the general "Objects and Plan" of the INSTITUTE OF TECHNOLOGY, proposed to be established, if practicable, on the Back-Bay lands in this city.

It is now proposed to hold a meeting in Mercantile Hall, 16, Summer Street, on Friday evening, 11th inst., at half-past seven o'clock, for the purpose of adopting measures preliminary to the organization of the Institute, and in furtherance of a petition to the Legislature for a Charter, and a portion of the Back-Bay lands.

As it is of the highest importance that the industrial and educational interests of the Commonwealth be amply represented at the meeting, we earnestly beg that you will favor us with your presence and counsel on that occasion. Should you be unable, however, to attend, but be desirous of co-operating, as a member of the Institute, in the great public objects we have in view, please affix your signature to the accompanying statement, and return the same, prior to the day of meeting, to the undersigned.

WILLIAM B. ROGERS, *Chairman of Committee.*

1, TEMPLE PLACE.

JANUARY , 1861.

The undersigned approves of the objects and general plan of the proposed INSTITUTE of TECHNOLOGY, and desires to have his name placed on its list of prospective members.

Previous to the day of meeting, replies were received from a large number of those to whom the pamphlet and circular had been addressed, requesting that they might be enrolled among the prospective members of the Institute, and otherwise indicating their hearty interest in the objects and action of the Committee.

The meeting was held at the appointed time; and after an exposition, by the Chairman, of the previous action and future purposes of the Committee, and interesting addresses by Prof. Peirce, Rev. Dr. Gannett, and others, in behalf of the Institute, a preliminary organization was established by adopting the following form of Association, to which the names of those present were affixed: —

"We the subscribers, feeling a deep interest in promoting the Industrial Arts and Sciences as well as Practical Education, heartily approve the objects and plan of an Institute of Technology, embracing a Society of Arts, a Museum of Arts, and a School of Industrial Science, as set forth in the Report of the Committee; and we hereby associate ourselves for the purpose of endeavoring to organize and establish in the city of Boston such an Institution, under the title of 'The Massachusetts Institute of Technology,' whensoever we may be legally empowered and properly prepared to carry these objects into effect."

The following resolutions were then adopted: —

"*Resolved,* That a Committee of twenty, with power to increase their number, be appointed to represent the interests and objects of the Association, and to act generally in its behalf, until it shall be legally incorporated and regularly organized under the title, and according to the purposes, of the Massachusetts Institute of Technology.

"*Resolved,* That said Committee be instructed to use its best efforts, in co-operation with the Committee of Associated Institutions of Science and Arts, to obtain from the Legislature an Act of Incorporation for the Institute, and to secure a grant of land on the Back Bay for its use, and for that of other institutions devoted to the Practical Sciences.

"*Resolved, further,* That this Committee be requested to frame a Constitution and By-laws for the government of said Institute in its several departments, and to submit the same to the consideration of this Association, whensoever we may be in readiness, and properly empowered, to organize formally as the Institute of Technology."

Subsequently, on motion, the Chairman of the meeting was added to the Committee, to act as its Chairman.

The members of this Committee are as follow: —

W. B. ROGERS, *Chairman.*

J. M. Beebe.	J. B. Francis.
E. S. Tobey.	J. C. Hoadley.
S. H. Gookin.	M. P. Wilder.
E. B. Bigelow.	C. L. Flint.
M. D. Ross.	Thos. Rice.
J. D. Philbrick.	John Chase.
F. S. Storer.	J. P. Robinson.
J. D. Runkle.	F. W. Lincoln, Jun.
C. H. Dalton.	Thos. Aspinwall.
E. C. Cabot.	J. S. Dupee.

LIST OF MEMBERS

OF THE

MASSACHUSETTS INSTITUTE OF TECHNOLOGY

THUS FAR ASSOCIATED.

William B. Rogers	Boston.
Samuel H. Gookin	"
Marshall P. Wilder	"
M. D. Ross	"
Alex. H. Rice	"
E. S. Tobey	"
James M. Beebe	"
Dr. S. Cabot, jun.	"
G. W. Pratt	"
Amos Binney	"
Dr. S. Kneeland, jun.	"
Charles L. Flint	"
B. S. Rotch	"
J. D. Philbrick	"
Geo. B. Emerson	"
Rev. R. C. Waterston	"
Erastus B. Bigelow	"
Chas. H. Dalton	"
Alfred Ordway	"
Dr. Henry I. Bowditch	"
James L. Little	"
John Lowell	"
R. M. Copeland	"
Dr. B. J. Jeffries	"
Thos. T. Bouvé	"
Dr. A. A. Gould	"

John Cummings, jun.	Woburn.
George W. Bond	Boston.
Dr. Geo. Hayward	„
E. B. Elliot	„
Andrew H. Ward, jun.	„
Chas. McBurney	„
Mertoun C. Bryant	Lowell.
William Boott	Boston.
Francis Alger	„
R. B. Forbes	„
O. H. Perry	Lowell.
F. P. Appleton	„
H. N. Bigelow	Clinton.
John Chase	Chicopee.
Hon. R. C. Winthrop	Boston.
Henry A. Peirce	„
Hon. F. W. Lincoln, jun..	„
Benj. Sewall	„
Moses Day	„
W. W. Greenough	„
Theodore Lyman	„
N. A. Thompson	„
Wm. Amory	„
H. P. Sturgis	„
E. Richmond	Brookline.
D. L. Webster	Boston.
John H. Wilkins	„
Zachary Allen	Providence.
Dr. Jacob Bigelow	Boston.
Frank S. Storer	„
John B. Henck	„
Andrew T. Hall	„
J. H. Blake	„
Thomas Lamb	„
Hon. G. W. Warren	Charlestown
Stephen Fairbanks	Boston.
R. C. Greenleaf	„
C. Allen Browne	„
James Ritchie	„
Dr. A. A. Hayes	„

Wm. A. Richardson	Lowell.
Jos. N. Howe	Boston.
Geo. M. Dexter	"
Thos. Sherwin	"
Dr. Chas. E. Ware	"
J. Russel Jencks	"
Carlos Pierce	"
John T. Heard	"
Dr. Geo. W. Dennet	"
C. H. Waters	Clinton.
Geo. M. Atwater	Springfield.
Thos. D. Shimmin	Boston.
Chas. F. Shimmin	"
G. H. Shaw	"
James Savage, jun.	"
Edward S. Rand	"
J. A. Higginson	"
Dr. Henry Wheatland	Salem.
Amos A. Lawrence	Boston.
David Sears, jun.	"
J. J. Dixwell	"
A. M. Gay	"
E. S. Ritchie	"
Richard Whitten	"
O. W. Peabody	"
James Edward Oliver	Lynn.
Alpheus Crosby	Salem.
L. C. Parton	Holyoke.
Sanborne Tenny	Auburndale.
D. E. Eddy	Boston.
James Hayward	"
W. C. Cabot	"
Edward S. Philbrick	"
Otis Clapp	"
E. Ritchie Dorr	"
D. W. Holmes	Cambridge.
Geo. F. Haskins	Boston.
D. G. Lang	Lowell.
Joshua G. Wilbur	Boston.
Col. Thos. Aspinwall	"

J. N. Turner . . . . Brookline.
Dr. C. T. Jackson . . . . Boston.
Wm. Edson . . . . „
J. Herbert Shedd . . . . „
George Snell . . . . „
John Stevens . . . . „
Dr. John Homans . . . . „
James S. Munroe . . . . Lexington, Mass.
W. H. Brooks . . . . Boston.
James A. Dupee . . . . „
Henry K. Oliver . . . . Salem.
Dr. Nathaniel B. Shurtleff . . . . Boston.
Edward Atkinson . . . . „
Jos. S. Fay . . . . „
Jas. McGregor . . . . „
R. M. Mason . . . . „
Chas. Nowell . . . . „
Avery Plumer . . . . „
Joseph C. Delano . . . . New Bedford.
John G. Webster . . . . Boston.
Alfred A. Hall . . . . „
J. Baxter . . . . „
Edward C. Cabot . . . . „
Dr. John Ware . . . . „
James B. Francis . . . . Lowell.
J. W. J. Jenks . . . . Middleborough.
W. H. Leany . . . . Boston.
Dr. Chas. D. Homans . . . . „
Henry B. Rogers . . . . „
John Duncan . . . . „
W. J. Whitwell . . . . „
Geo. B. Upton . . . . „
Samuel H. Walley . . . . „
Dr. Thomas M. Brewer . . . . „
Greely S. Curtis . . . . „
Patrick Riley . . . . „
C. M. Warren . . . . „
Ch. K. Dillaway . . . . „
Rev. Chas. F. Barnard . . . . „
Henry J. Tudor . . . . „

Aaron P. Richardson	Boston.
James Dennie	„
Franklin Forbes	Clinton.
Prof. Bowen	Cambridge.
Prof. Pierce	„
Pres. Felton	„
Prof. Horsford	„
Prof. Eliot	„
Hon. Joel Parker	„
Rev. Dr. Blagden	Boston.
W. S. Bullard	„
Thos. H. Blake	„
Jas. C. Converse	„
Hon. Jona. Preston	„
Rev. Ezra S. Gannett	„
Aug. A. Noyes	„
Sidney Homer	„
Henry Williams	„
Geo. W. Tuxbury	„
H. Bigelow	„
John C. Dalton	„
Dr. Samuel A. Green	„
Geo. Odiorne	„
Levi L. Willcutt	„
Wm. P. Parrott	„
Dr. Wm. E. Coale	„
J. D. Runkle	Dedham.
David Bryant	Boston.
Chas. W. Folsom	„
James Slade	„
Chas. B. Hall	„
Edwin P. Whipple	„
Zoheth S. Durfee	New Bedford.
Joseph E. Brown	Boston.
Chas. H. Bigelow	New Bedford.
Chas. G. Loring	Boston.
Prof. Oliver W. Holmes	„
Hon. Emory Washburn	Cambridge.
David Buck	Boston.
Causten Browne	„

J. Huntington Wolcott . . . . Boston.
Samuel Hooper . . . . ,,
C. R. Mower . . . . ,,
Thomas Boyd . . . . ,,
Alex. R. Esty . . . . ,,
Rev. Andrew Bigelow . . . . ,,
Rev. Wm. R. Alger. . . . . ,,
Edward Atkinson . . . . ,,
G. W. Briggs . . . . Auburndale.
Hon. John P. Putnam . . . . Boston.
Dr. Geo. H. Lyman . . . . ,,
Dr. John B. Alley . . . . ,,
C. C. Jewett . . . . ,,
Dr. Henry W. Williams . . . . ,,
John Pearce . . . . ,,
Alfred Peabody . . . . Salem.
Joseph Vila, jun. . . . . Roxbury.
Edward Hixon . . . . Cambridge.
D. Sparhawk . . . . Boston.
A. W. Spencer . . . . Dorchester.
Jas. P. Farley . . . . Chelsea.
Hon. Geo. P. Sanger . . . . Boston.
John C. Boyd . . . . ,,

APPENDIX.

MEMORIAL

OF THE

Committee of Associated Institutions of Science and Arts.

1861.

THE undersigned, a Committee representing various Institutions devoted to Science and the Arts, have been instructed to memorialize your honorable body, to the effect as follows: —

First, That you will be pleased to grant to the Association of Industrial Art and Science, recently formed, a Charter and corporate existence, under the title of the "Massachusetts Institute of Technology," empowering it to carry into effect the plan and purposes of a Society of Arts, a Museum of Arts, and a School of Industrial Science, as set forth in the Report prepared by your memorialists, and herewith submitted.

Second, That you will set apart and assign a portion of the Back-Bay lands, in a continuous space, for the use and accommodation of the Boston Society of Natural History, the Massachusetts Horticultural Society, and the above-named Institute of Technology, under such conditions as in your judgment may best promote the practical objects of these Institutions, and conduce to the educational and industrial interests of the Commonwealth.

For the details of the organization and purposes of these several societies, and of their claims upon your favorable consideration as connected with the science, industry, and education of the State, your memorialists beg to call your attention to the printed pamphlets and other documents herewith submitted to your inspection.

In regard to the previous action of the Legislature on this subject, your memorialists would beg to state, that, two years ago, they submitted to your honorable body a petition of like general import with the present, which was reported on favorably by the Committee to whom it was referred; that they renewed their application, in a more specific shape, to the last General Court; and that the bill reported to the lower House, and rejected by the Senate at the close of the session, was, on motion to reconsider, laid upon the table.

Your memorialists deem it important to add, that during the past year, while endeavoring to make their plans widely known throughout the Commonwealth, and while maturing an organization for the proposed Institute of Technology, they have received from various quarters the amplest evidences of public approbation and sympathy, not only towards the last-named feature of the plan, but in regard to the objects and claims of the Boston Society of Natural History and the Massachusetts Horticultural Society, in connection with the general purpose of a collocation of these and kindred Institutions in a continuous space upon the Back-Bay lands.

Your memorialists, therefore, feel no hesitation in renewing their application to your honorable body, in a modified and more perfect form; trusting the issue to your wise judgment of the merits of their plan, and to the ever-recognized claims of education, industry, and science upon the fostering favor of the State.

WILLIAM B. ROGERS, *Chairman*.

Marshall P. Wilder,
Samuel H. Gookin,
M. D. Ross,
B. S. Rotch,
R. C. Waterston,
Alfred Ordway,
Alex. H. Rice,
E. S. Tobey,
James M. Beebe,
Dr. S. Cabot, Jun.,
G. W. Pratt,
Amos Binney,
Dr. S. Kneeland, Jun.,
Charles L. Flint,
J. D. Philbrick,
Geo. B. Emerson,
Erastus B. Bigelow,
Charles H. Dalton,

Committee.

PETITIONS IN AID.

BOSTON SOCIETY OF NATURAL HISTORY.

To the Honorable Senate and House of Representatives of the Commonwealth of Massachusetts, in General Court assembled.

THE Boston Society of Natural History joins in the memorial of the Committee of citizens of the Commonwealth, whereof Marshall P. Wilder is Chairman, asking for a reservation of land from the Commonwealth's territory on the Back Bay, for the use of Associated Institutions of Science and Art; and petitions your honorable body, that the prayer of the said memorial may be granted.

And the said Boston Society of Natural History respectfully represents, in its own behalf, that the great value and purely disinterested character of the services which it has already rendered during the past thirty years, and which it is still rendering, to the cause of liberal education in this Commonwealth, as is fully set forth in the said memorial, constitute a pre-eminent title to such aid and encouragement from the State, in extending and perpetuating its usefulness, as is contemplated in the said memorial.

JEFFRIES WYMAN,
Pres. of the Boston Society of Nat. History.

BOSTON, Jan. 12, 1860.

BOSTON BOARD OF TRADE.

To the Honorable the Senate and House of Representatives o Massachusetts, in General Court assembled.

The Boston Board of Trade would hereby respectfully petition in aid of a memorial now before your honorable body; in which a Committee, representing the interests of Agriculture, Horticulture, Natural Sciences, Commerce, Manufactures, the Mechanic and Fine Arts, and General Education, ask for a reservation of a portion of the Back-Bay lands, for the use of Associated Institutions engaged in promoting these several interests.

While this Board cannot be indifferent to the general plan, and all the objects indicated in the memorial already referred to, its interest has special reference to the department which pertains to Commerce and Manufactures, the promotion of which is one of the principal objects of its organization. The necessity and value, to the community, of Institutions like those contemplated in the memorial, must be obvious; and their influence will have a tendency to aid in widely diffusing amongst the masses of our population valuable and practical knowledge, and thus promote the welfare and prosperity of the State.

Your petitioners would, therefore, earnestly request the favorable attention of your honorable body to the memorial, and would respectfully ask that its objects may be granted.

LORENZO SABINE, *Secretary.*
E. S. TOBEY, *President.*

Office, Board of Trade, Boston, Feb. 6, 1860.

AMERICAN ACADEMY OF ARTS AND SCIENCES.

THE American Academy of Arts and Sciences respectfully and urgently recommend to the favorable consideration of your honorable body the petition of Marshall P. Wilder and others in behalf of Associated Institutions of Arts and Science, asking for a reservation of Back-Bay lands, &c.

They do this because, in their judgment, the measure prayed for would tend directly and strongly to promote the scientific, the educational, and the industrial interests of the Commonwealth.

Because it would be a testimony to the public benefit, derivable from the acquisition, the diffusion, and the use of knowledge, which would be alike honorable to the Legislature and the Commonwealth.

Because it would receive the approbation of all who know — and they will be all who inquire into the facts — that the institutions which it proposes to assist are actively engaged in scientific discovery, and in efforts to learn all that is discovered elsewhere; and to apply all knowledge, as far as possible, to the various industrial pursuits, upon the success of which depends the prosperity, not only of those engaged in them, but of all who are in any way connected with the persons so employed; and, therefore, of the State.

Because they regard it as a measure which will harmonize and co-operate with all those which have been or can be adopted for general education; and will concur with them in providing such means of mental improvement, that every mind may have its due development, and no talent be wasted and suppressed because the means for its culture and exercise are not within its reach; and will assist in offering to every man an opportunity of becoming all that his capacity, and his willingness to improve and use his capacity, permit him to be. And they regard this as the end which must be reached before the educational system of Massachusetts can be considered as complete.

All which is respectfully submitted by the Fellows of the Academy, through the undersigned, who are a Committee appointed for this purpose.

THEOPHILUS PARSONS.
CHARLES G. LORING.
CHARLES JACKSON, Jun.

BOSTON, Feb. 18, 1860.

MASSACHUSETTS CHARITABLE MECHANICS' ASSOCIATION.

To the Honorable the Senate and House of Representatives, in General Court assembled.

THE undersigned, the Government of the Massachusetts Charitable Mechanics' Association, would respectfully petition your honorable body in aid of a "Memorial" now before the Legislature, asking for a grant of land on the Back Bay for the use of the Associated Institutions of Science and Art. Fully approving the general plan as a means of public education of inestimable value, the Society we represent feels a special and lively interest in the Third Section, in which would be associated the Institutions cultivating the Mechanic Arts. Knowing by experience the advantages of mutual interchange of ideas in the advancement of the mechanic arts, and conscious of the disadvantage we labor under for the want of Polytechnic Institutions which shall bring Science and Art into closer communion, we shall hail with pleasure and satisfaction the establishment of such as this memorial proposes on Section Three.

Believing that the objects of our organization, and the interests of the Mechanic Arts throughout the State, would be promoted by the reservation asked for, we would earnestly request your favororable consideration of the prayer of the petitioners; and, as in duty bound, will ever pray.

PELHAM BONNEY, *President.*

FRED. H. STIMPSON.	NATH. ADAMS.
AL. SANBORN.	L. MILES STANDISH.
WM. W. WHEILDON.	JOSEPH L. BATES.
CHARLES WOODBURY.	JAMES TOLMAN.
OSMYN BREWSTER.	J. C. HUBBARD.
JOS. T. BAILEY.	ANSEL LOTHROP.

NEW-ENGLAND SOCIETY.

To the Honorable the Senate and House of Representatives of Massachusetts, in General Court assembled.

THE New-England Society for the Promotion of Manufactures and Mechanic Arts, instituted for the purpose of diffusing knowledge in these important branches of American industry, would respectfully petition your honorable body in aid of a memorial presented to the Legislature by a Committee of gentlemen representing the various Associations of Science and the Arts, whereof the Hon. Marshall P. Wilder is Chairman, asking for a reservation of land on the Back Back, in the city of Boston, for the use of the Associated Institutions.

The New-England Society finds the subject very ably presented in the above memorial now before your honorable body, and entirely approves of the arguments therein contained; and, should the reservation be made, will endeavor to make the department in which its members are interested a benefit and an honor to the State.

Your petitioners would respectfully represent that it comes within the especial province of this Society to aid in the establishment of such Institutions as are contemplated in the Third Section of the plan of the general memorial; namely, that relating to Mechanics, Manufactures, and Commerce. There can be no doubt, in our opinion, that a large space will in the future be needed for the uses of this department; and we fully concur in the views expressed in the memorial of the Committee, that at least one square will be necessary for the accommodation of the Institutions of Mechanics, Manufactures, and Commerce.

We would, therefore, respectfully and earnestly request that the petition of the general memorial may be granted; firmly believing that the industrial interests of the State, which we are instituted to promote, will be signally benefited by this act in all coming time.

DEMING JARVES, *President.*

J. Wiley Edmands.
Benj. E. Bates.
James Read.
Tyler Batcheller.
Thomas P. Rich.
Tho. Motley.

J. A. Lowell.
Henry J. Gardner.
E. H. Eldridge.
Amos A. Lawrence.
Jas. M. Beebe.
F. Skinner.

PETER BUTLER, *Secretary.*

STATE TEACHERS' ASSOCIATION.

At a meeting of the State Teachers' Association, held at Concord, December, 1860, the following resolutions were "cordially received and unanimously adopted:" —

Resolved, That this Association regards with hearty interest and sympathy the purposes set forth by the Committee of Associated Institutions of Science and Arts, acting in behalf of the Boston Society of Natural History, the Massachusetts Horticultural Society, and the Massachusetts Institute of Technology now about to be established, wherein it is proposed to enlarge the facilities of popular instruction in Natural Science and its applications, and to provide a system of education suited to the development of intelligent industry and the promotion of liberal culture in connection with industrial pursuits.

Resolved, That, in our opinion, the largest general benefits will be secured from the museums, conservatories, and other means of instruction, of these several institutions, not only by having them placed in the midst of the dense population, and facilities of access, of our metropolis, but by bringing them into relations of close proximity and mutual illustration; and that, therefore, we cordially approve the proposed plan of setting apart a continuous portion of the Back-Bay lands for their accommodation.

www.ingramcontent.com/pod-product-compliance
Lightning Source LLC
LaVergne TN
LVHW011140110826
845150LV00008B/2433

* 9 7 8 1 4 1 8 1 9 3 3 3 1 *